THE WHISKEY JOURNAL

FOR DOCUMENTING YOUR WHISKEY TASTING ADVENTURES

THE GOLDEN AGE OF NOTEBOOKS™

ABOUT

THIS WHISKEY JOURNAL IS OWNED BY

IF THIS JOURNAL IS LOST, PLEASE BE SO KIND AS TO RETURN IT TO / CONTACT

REWARD
- ○ YES
- ○ NO
- ○ MAYBE

START DATE

END DATE

THE GOLDEN AGE OF NOTEBOOKS IS AN IMPRINT OF THE PRODUCTIVE LUDDITE. COPYRIGHT © 2013 THE PRODUCTIVE LUDDITE. VISIT: PRODUCTIVELUDDITE.COM

Any companies or products identified in this book are used in editorial fashion only and for the benefit of such companies with no intention of infringement of trademark or other rights. No such use, or the use of any trade name, is intended to convey endorsement or other affiliation with this book. The publishers and author of this book are not affiliated or associated with any website, company, product, or service mentioned in this book. All company names, product names and logos are the trademarks of their respective owners.

HOW TO USE THE WHISKEY JOURNAL

THE WHISKEY JOURNAL is used to record and track your adventures in whiskey tasting. There's room to keep tabs on your Whiskey Inventory, Favorite Whiskey, Whiskey Wish List, and the important details of the whiskies you encounter.

NAME	What is the name of the whiskey?
DISTILLER	Who made the whiskey?
COUNTRY	What country was the whiskey made in?
TYPE	What type of whiskey is it: Blended, Blended Malt, Bourbon, Cask Strength (Barrel Proof), Corn, Grain, Malt, Rye, Rye Malt, Single Cask (Single Barrel), Single Malt?
SIZE	What size was your whiskey? A glass? A 26 ounce bottle?
COST	What did the whiskey cost
AGED	How many years was the whiskey aged?
PROOF	What was the proof or percent alcohol of the whiskey?
RATING	In the rating's area there are five stars. How many stars do you give this whiskey?
BOUGHT: WHERE/WHEN	Where and when did you buy they whiskey?
DRANK: WHERE/WHEN	Where and when did you drink the whiskey
COLOR-THERMOMETER	On a scale of clear to black molasses, what color was the whiskey?
NOTES	Use the NOTES section to capture your impressions about the whiskey and anything related to it.
FLAVOR RADAR	Use the FLAVOR RADAR to create your own signature for each whiskey's flavour. This will help you recall and remember your impressions of the many different whiskies you review using The Whiskey Journal. Fill in the radar blips (dots) for each dimension of taste and connect them with a line. You may want to shade in the area for ease of visual reference. The result is your own unique signature radar pattern reflecting how you experienced the whiskey.

FLAVOR RADAR
CONNECT THE FLAVOR DOTS

Use the **FLAVOR RADAR** to create your own signature for each whiskey's flavour. This will help you recall and remember your impressions of the many different whiskies you review using **The Whiskey Journal**. Fill in the radar blips (dots) for each dimension of taste and connect them with a line. You may want to shade in the area for ease of visual reference. The result is your own unique signature radar pattern that reflects how you experienced the whiskey.

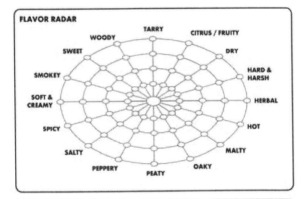

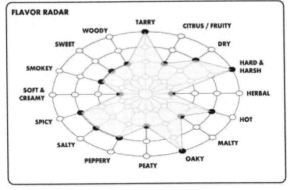

WHISKEY WISH LIST
WHISKEY + WHERE + COST + CHECK WHEN YOU GET IT

WHISKEY INVENTORY

WHISKEY	QUANTITY	DATE ACQUIRED	ALL GONE ✔
			☐
			☐
			☐
			☐
			☐
			☐
			☐
			☐
			☐
			☐
			☐
			☐
			☐
			☐
			☐
			☐
			☐

WHISKEY INVENTORY

WHISKEY	QUANTITY	DATE ACQUIRED	ALL GONE ✔
			☐
			☐
			☐
			☐
			☐
			☐
			☐
			☐
			☐
			☐
			☐
			☐
			☐
			☐
			☐
			☐
			☐

MY FAVORITE WHISKEY
BRAND + REASON

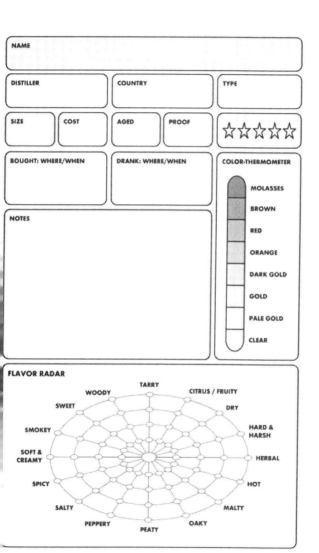

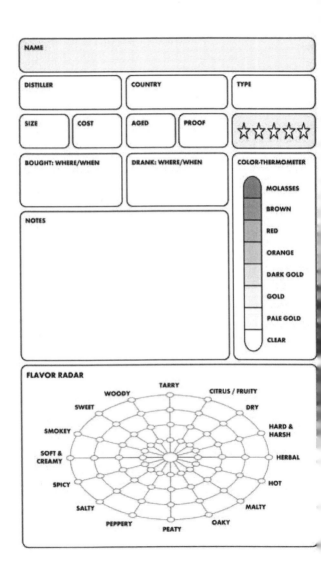

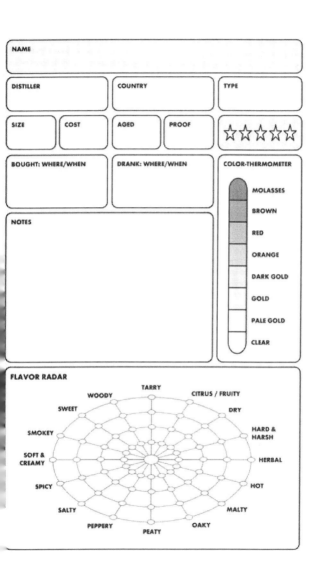

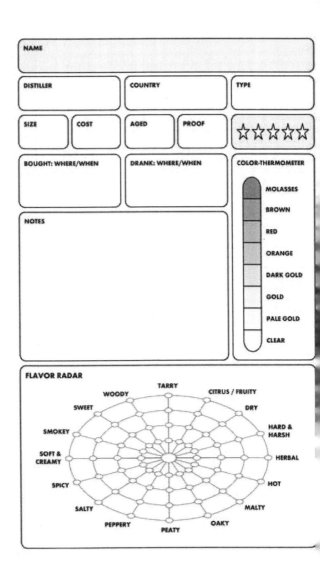

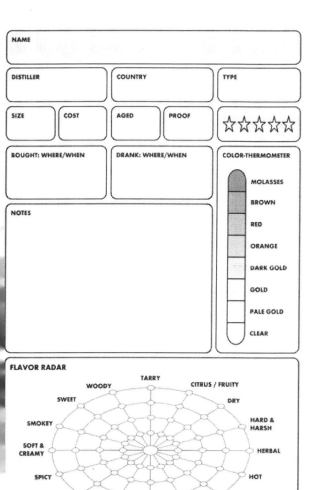

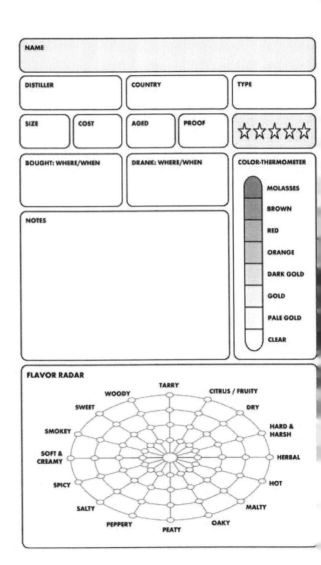

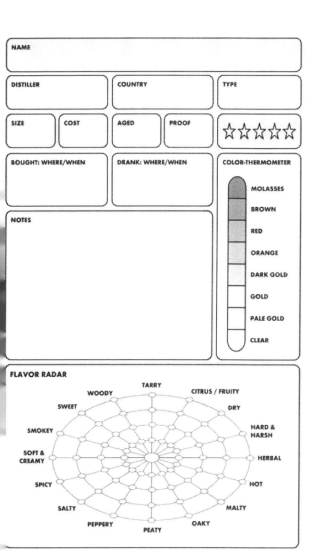

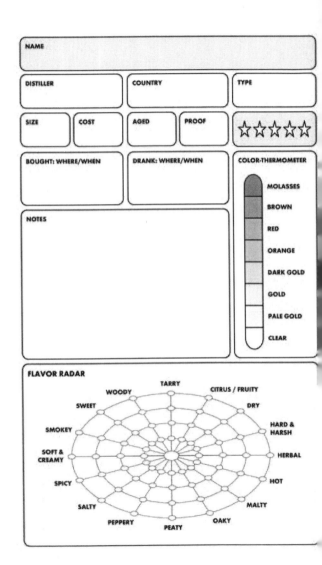

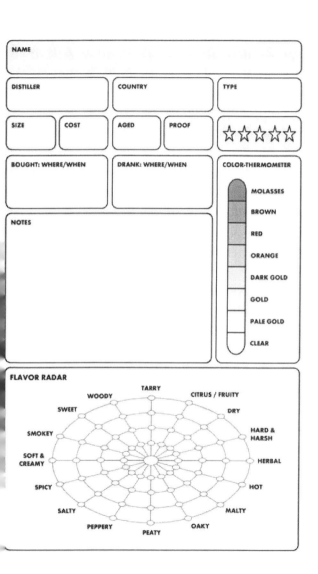

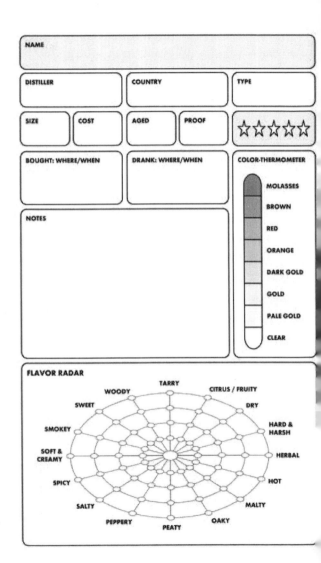

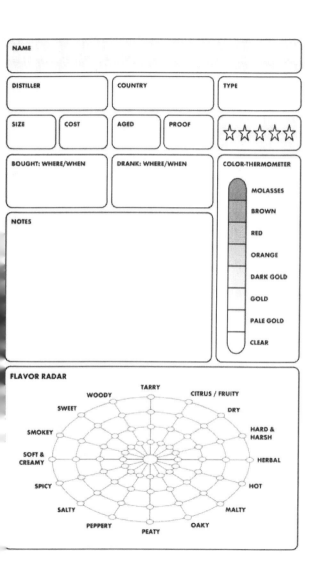

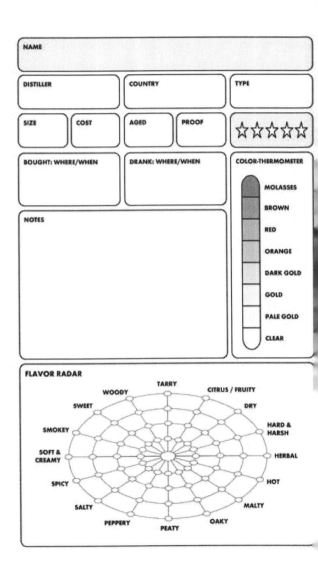

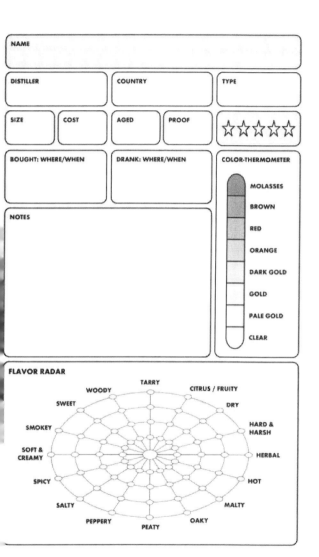

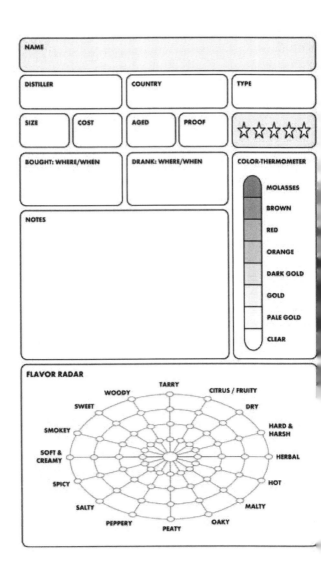

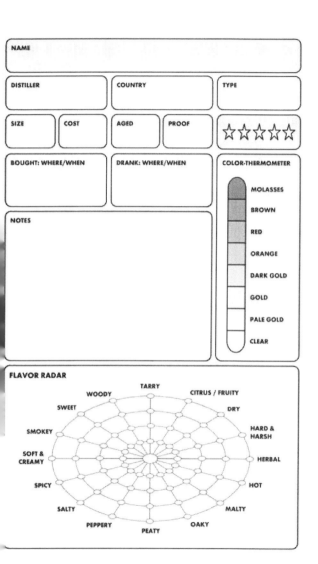

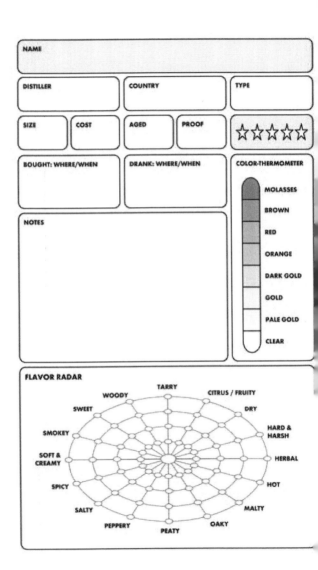

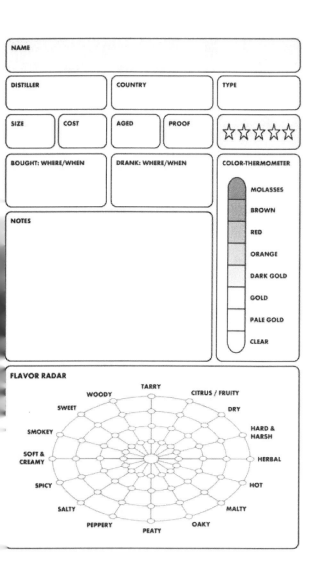

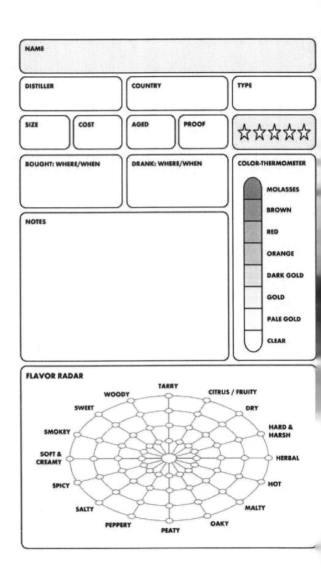

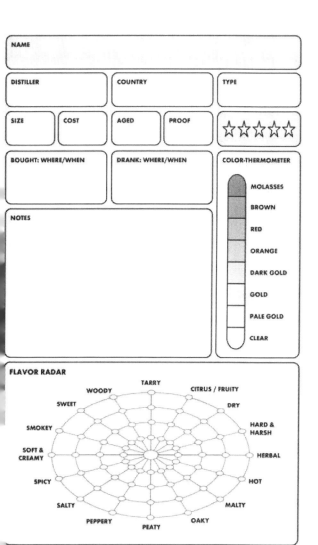

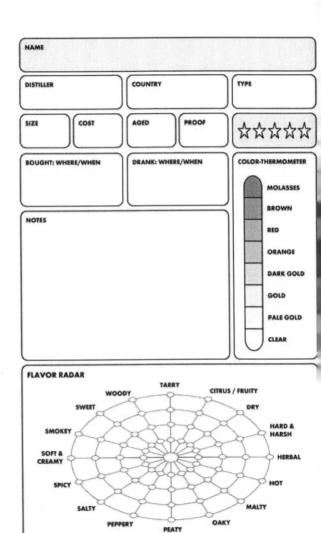

NAME

DISTILLER | **COUNTRY** | **TYPE**

SIZE | **COST** | **AGED** | **PROOF** | ☆☆☆☆☆

BOUGHT: WHERE/WHEN | **DRANK: WHERE/WHEN** | **COLOR-THERMOMETER**

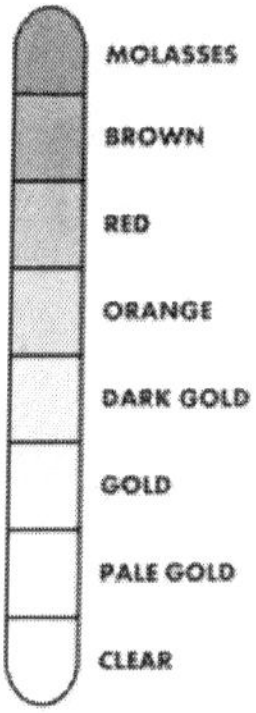

- MOLASSES
- BROWN
- RED
- ORANGE
- DARK GOLD
- GOLD
- PALE GOLD
- CLEAR

NOTES

FLAVOR RADAR

- TARRY
- WOODY
- CITRUS / FRUITY
- SWEET
- DRY
- SMOKEY
- HARD & HARSH
- SOFT & CREAMY
- HERBAL
- SPICY
- HOT
- SALTY
- MALTY
- PEPPERY
- PEATY
- OAKY

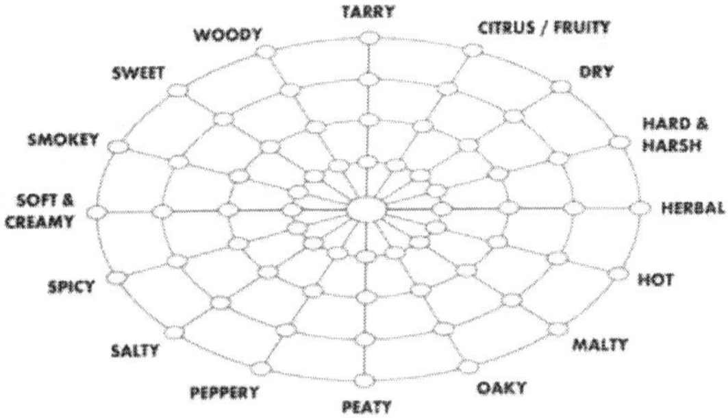

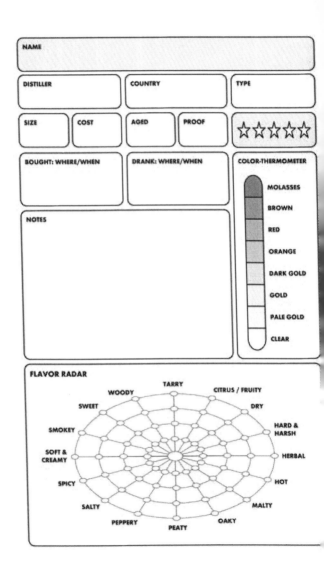

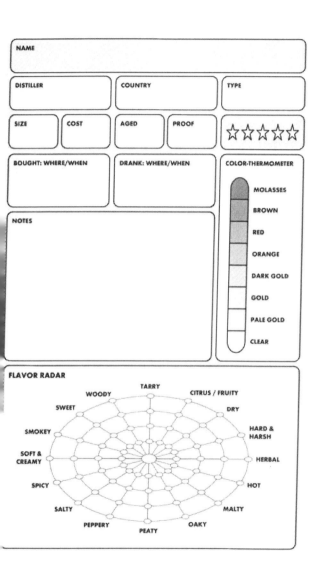

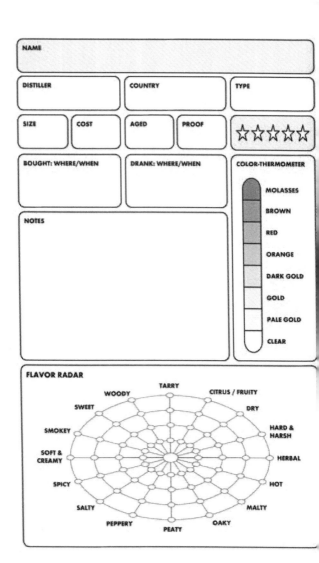

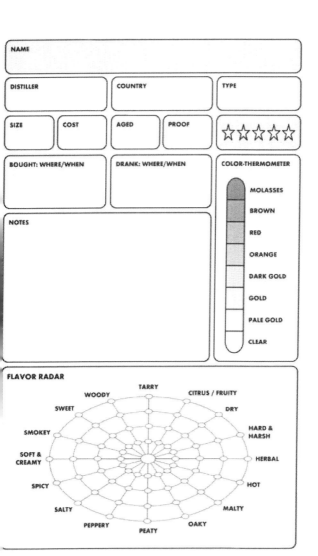

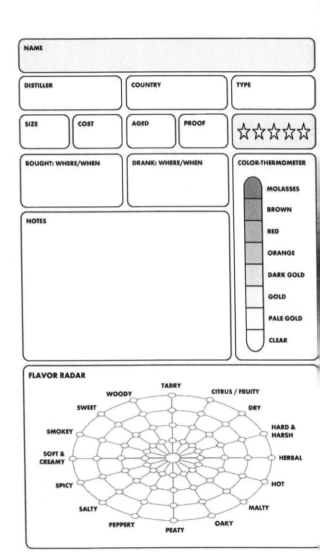

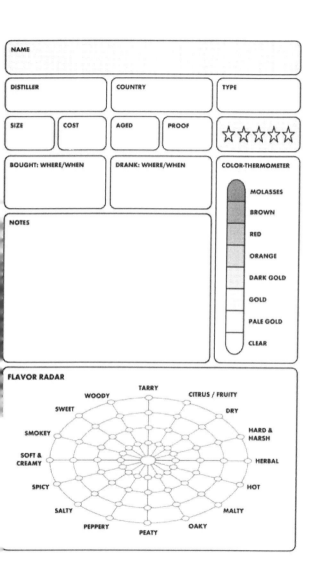

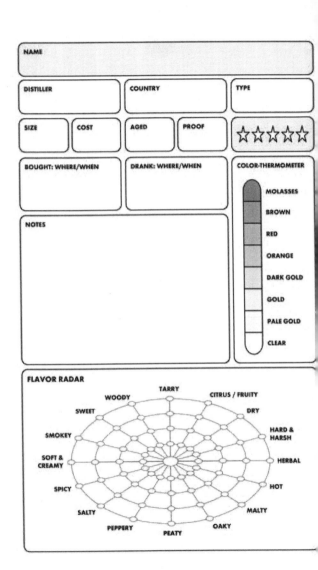

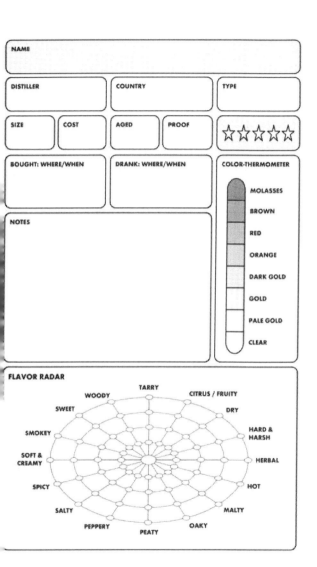

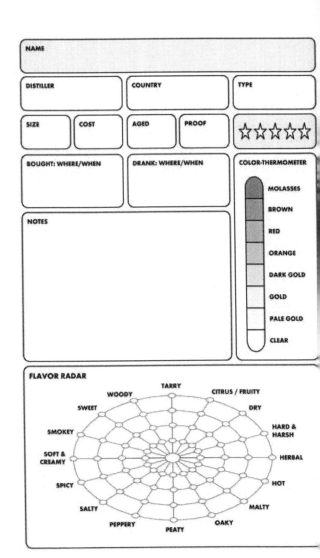

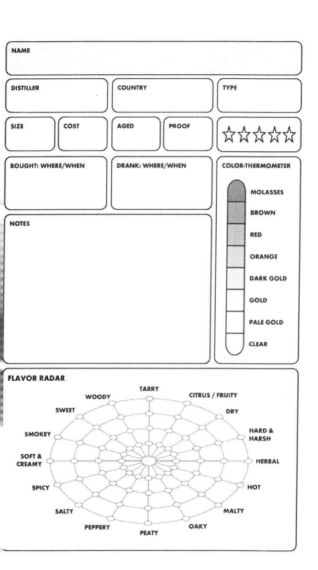

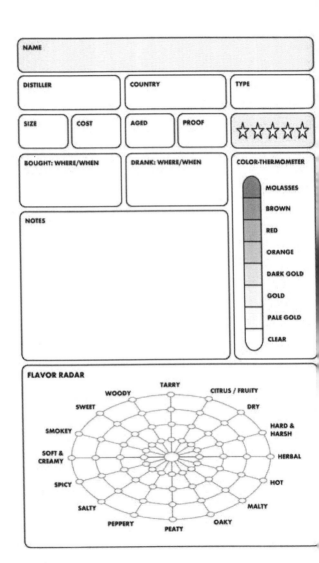

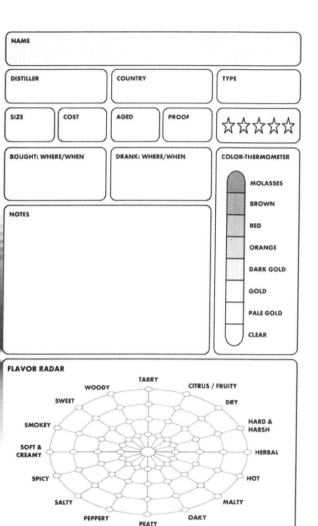

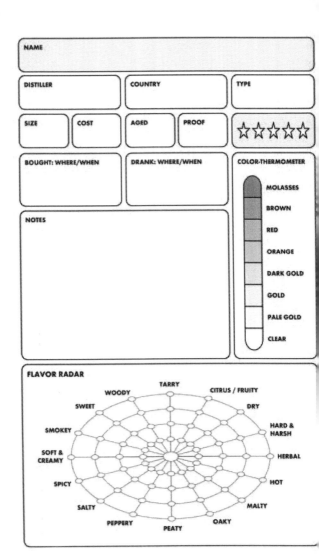

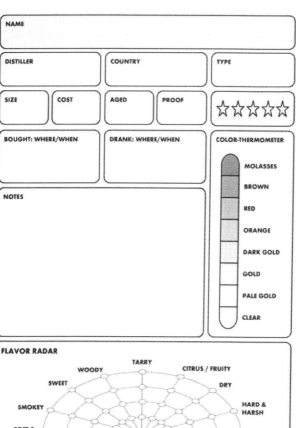
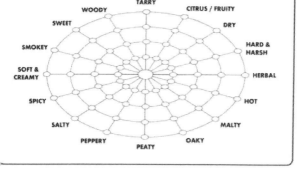

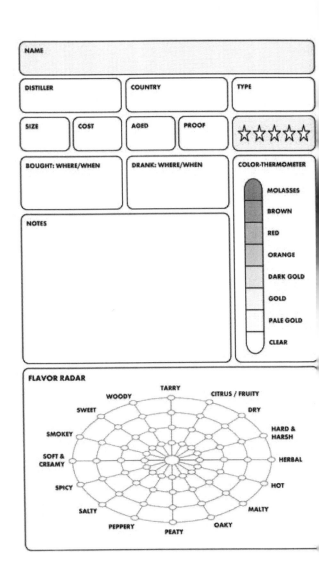

NAME

DISTILLER

COUNTRY

TYPE

SIZE　**COST**　**AGED**　**PROOF**

☆☆☆☆☆

BOUGHT: WHERE/WHEN

DRANK: WHERE/WHEN

COLOR-THERMOMETER

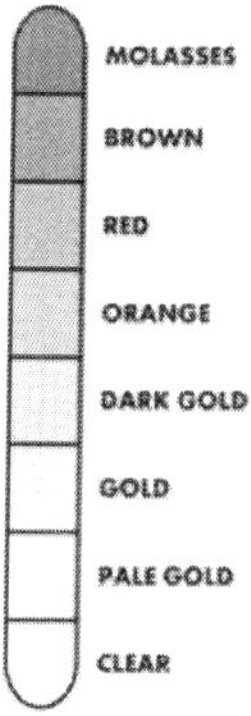

- MOLASSES
- BROWN
- RED
- ORANGE
- DARK GOLD
- GOLD
- PALE GOLD
- CLEAR

NOTES

FLAVOR RADAR

TARRY, WOODY, CITRUS / FRUITY, SWEET, DRY, SMOKEY, HARD & HARSH, SOFT & CREAMY, HERBAL, SPICY, HOT, SALTY, MALTY, PEPPERY, PEATY, OAKY

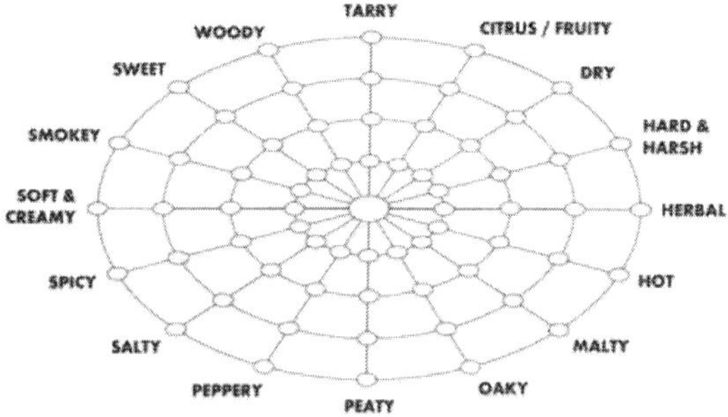

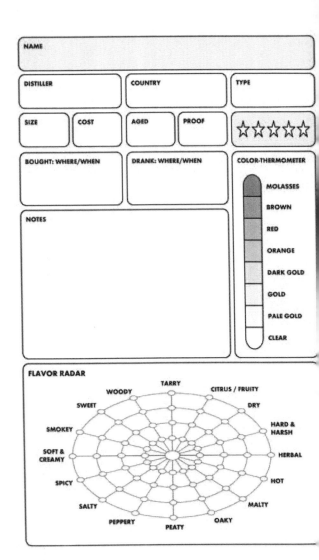

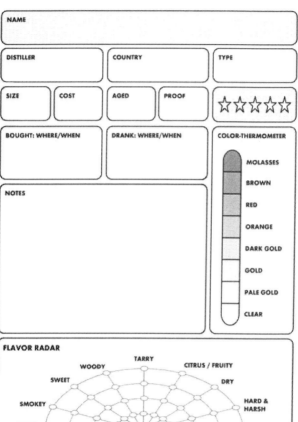

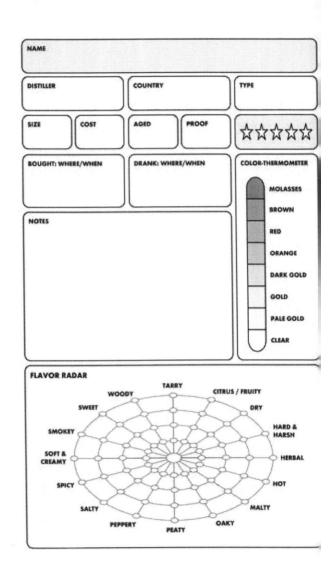

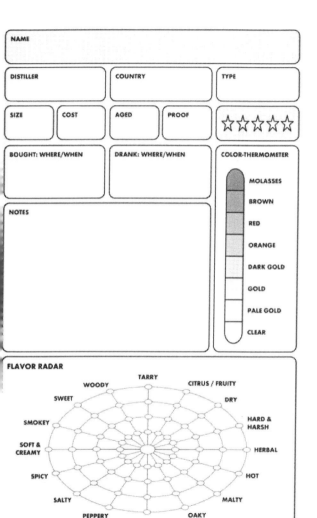

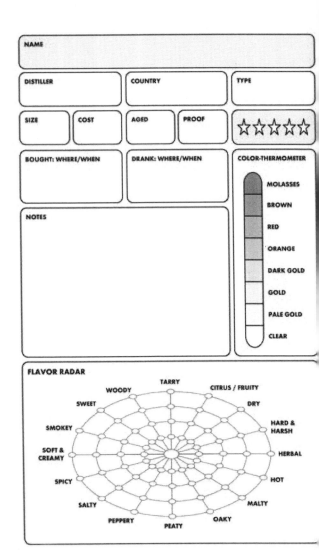

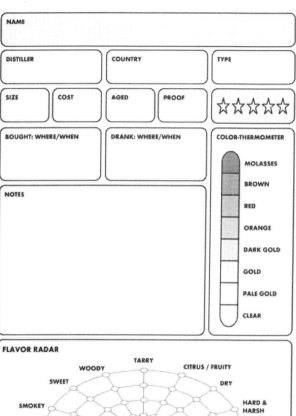

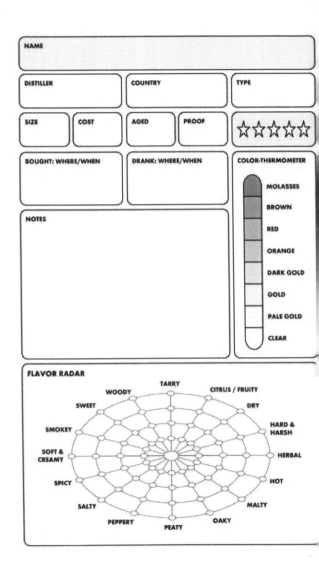

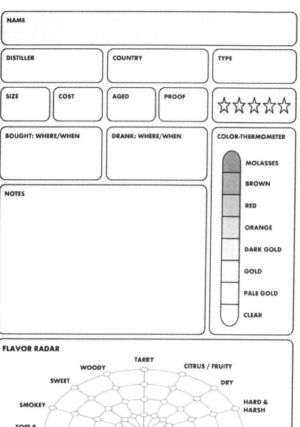
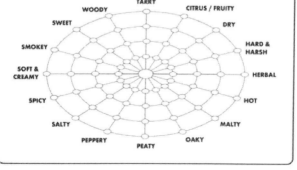

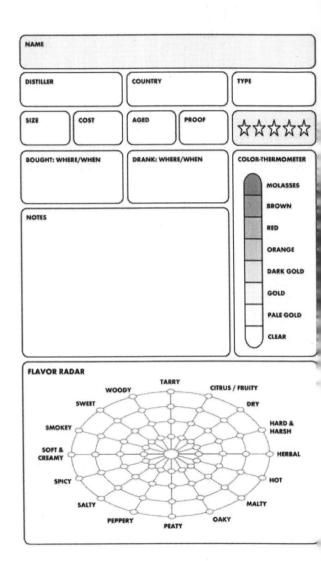

NAME

DISTILLER **COUNTRY** **TYPE**

SIZE **COST** **AGED** **PROOF** ☆☆☆☆☆

BOUGHT: WHERE/WHEN **DRANK: WHERE/WHEN** **COLOR-THERMOMETER**

- MOLASSES
- BROWN
- RED
- ORANGE
- DARK GOLD
- GOLD
- PALE GOLD
- CLEAR

NOTES

FLAVOR RADAR

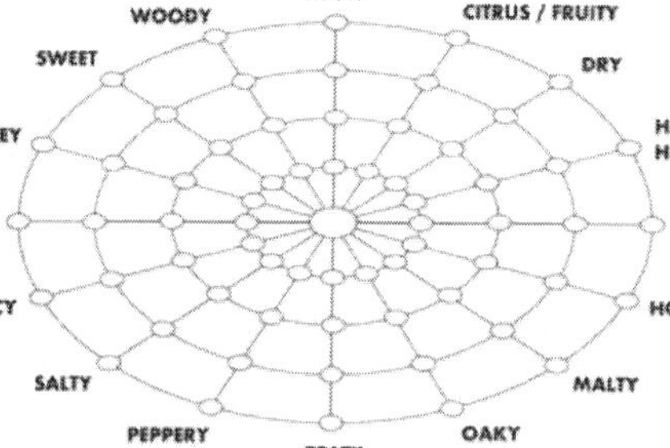

- TARRY
- WOODY
- CITRUS / FRUITY
- SWEET
- DRY
- SMOKEY
- HARD & HARSH
- SOFT & CREAMY
- HERBAL
- SPICY
- HOT
- SALTY
- MALTY
- PEPPERY
- OAKY
- PEATY

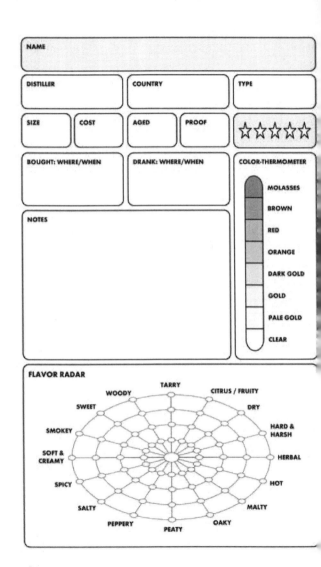

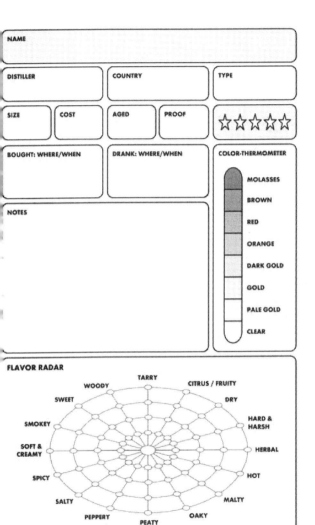

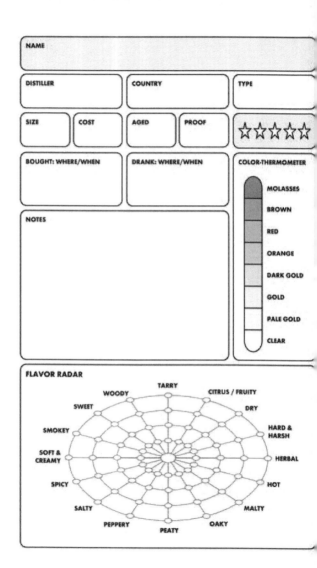

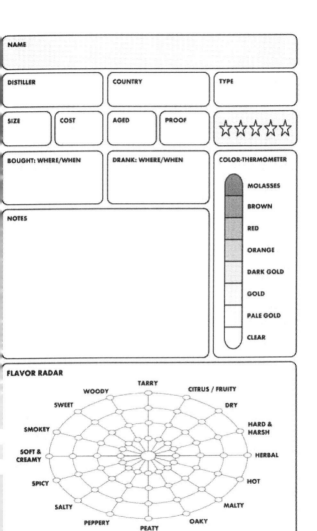

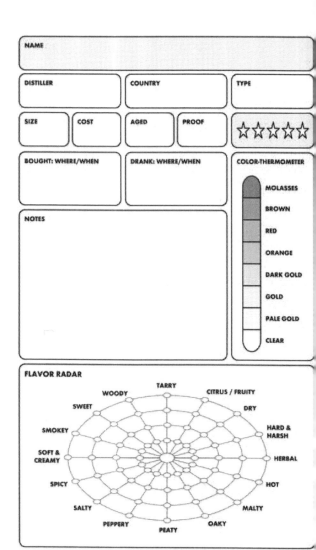

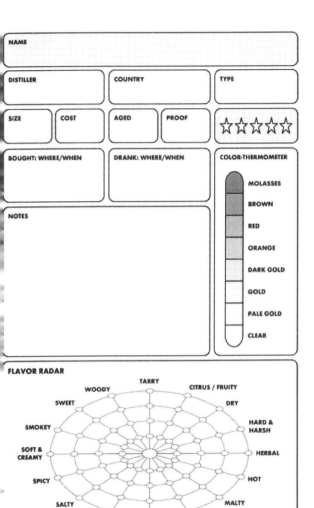

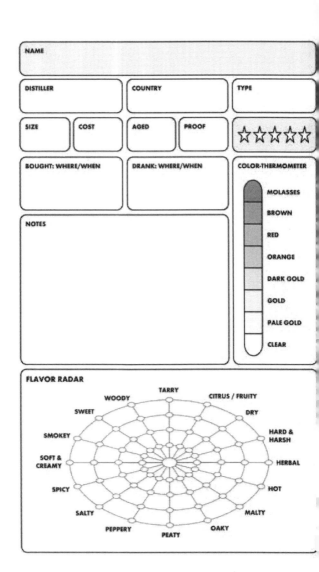

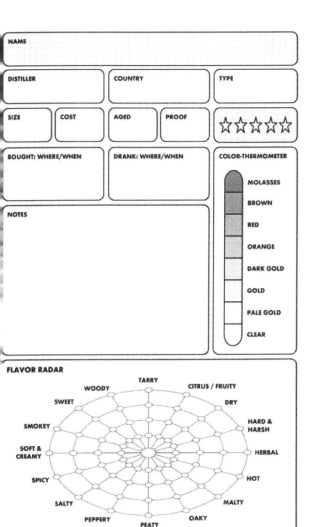

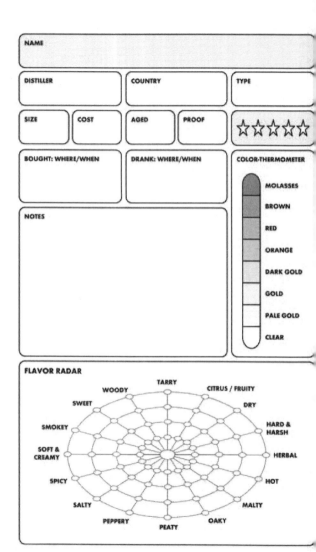

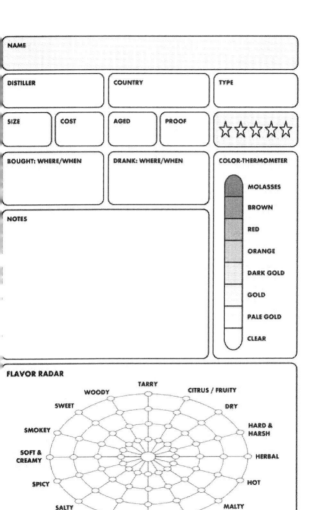

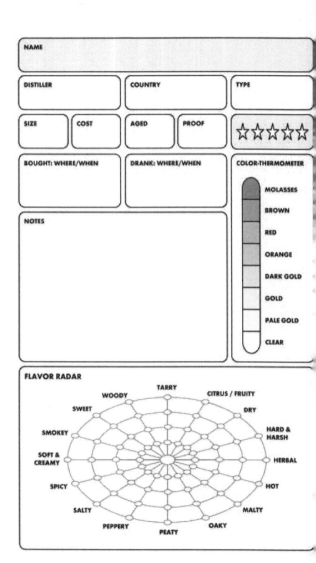

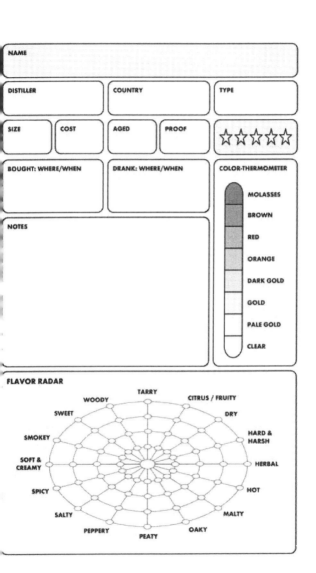

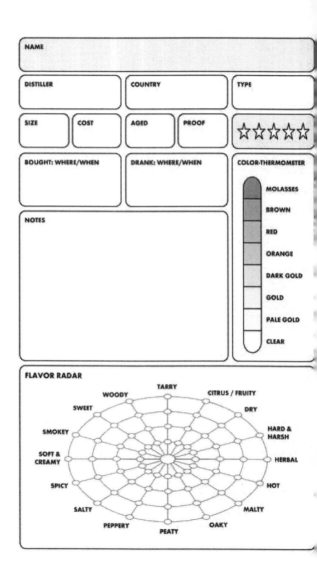

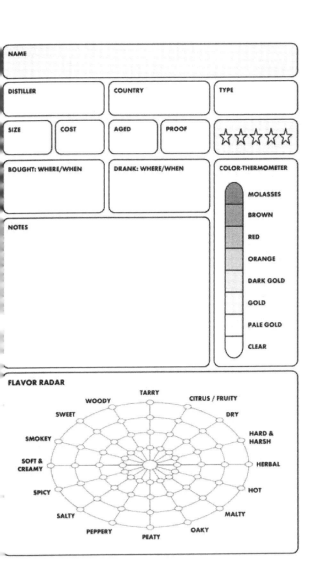

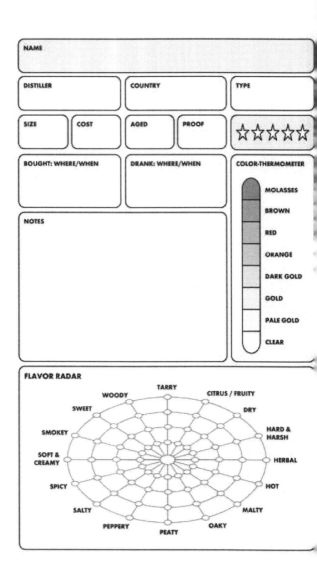

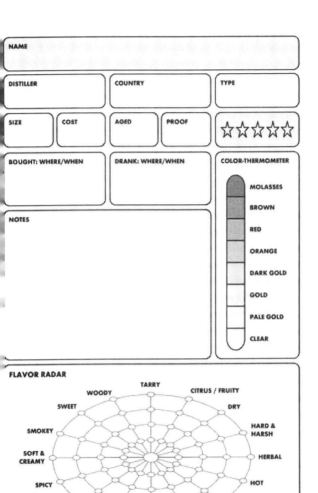

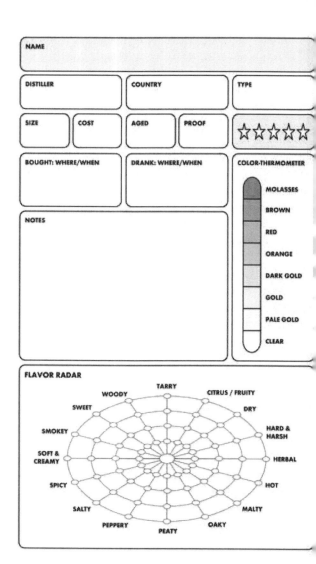

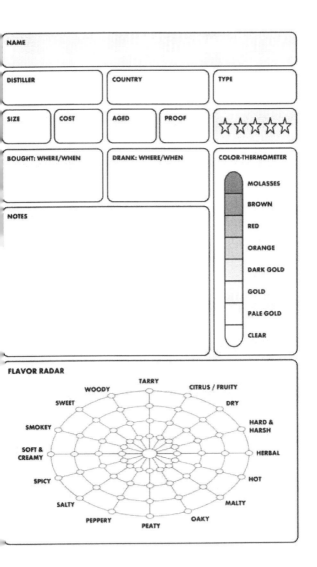

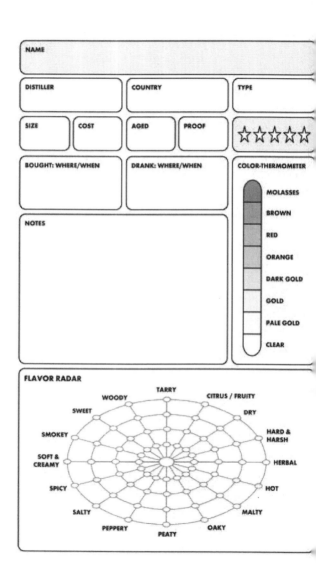

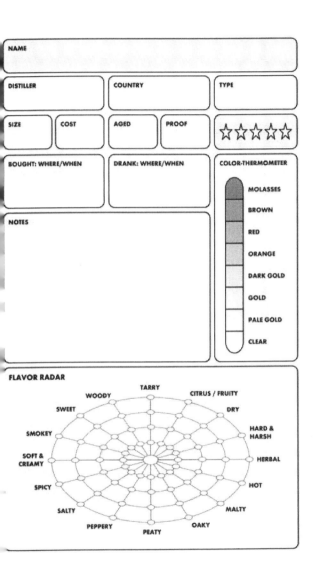

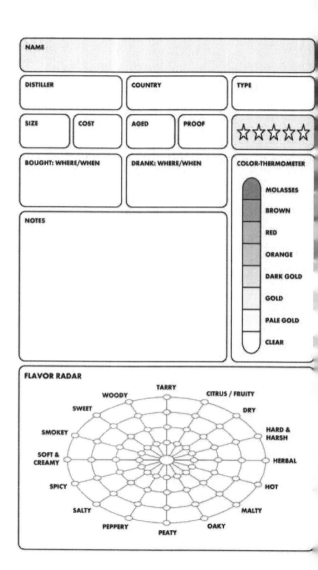

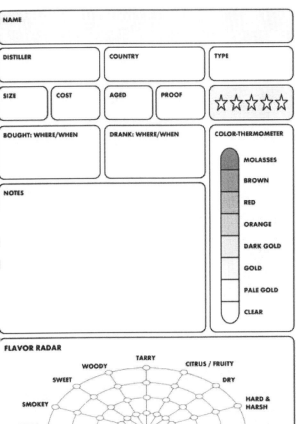
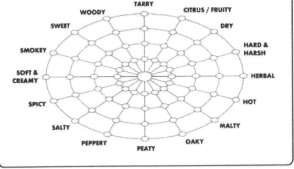

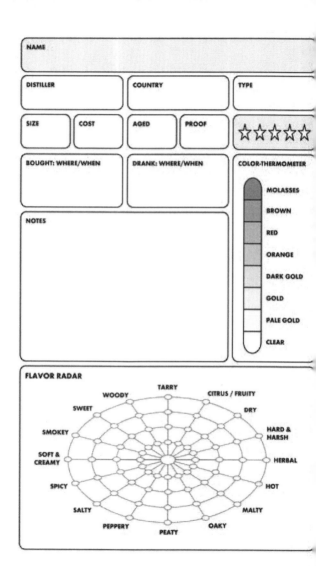

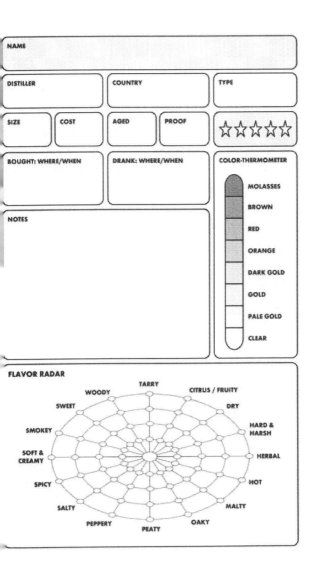

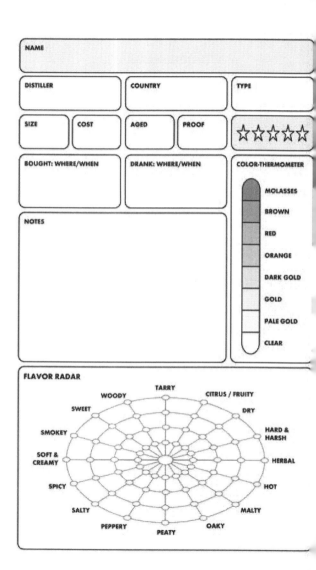

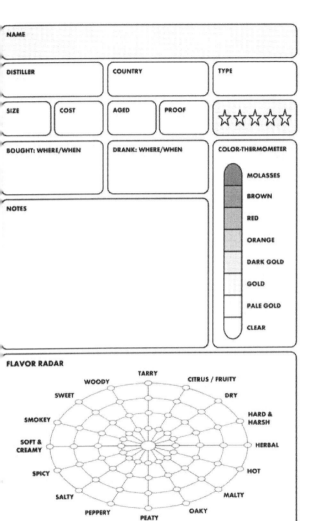

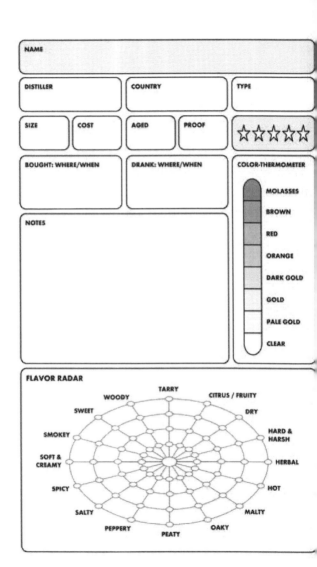

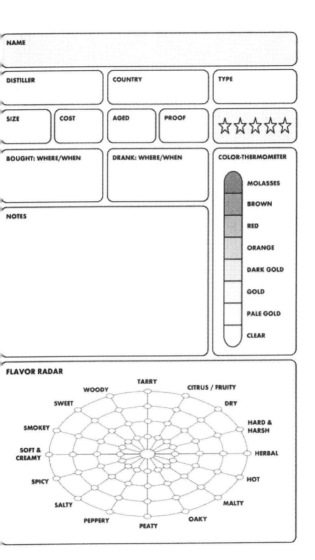

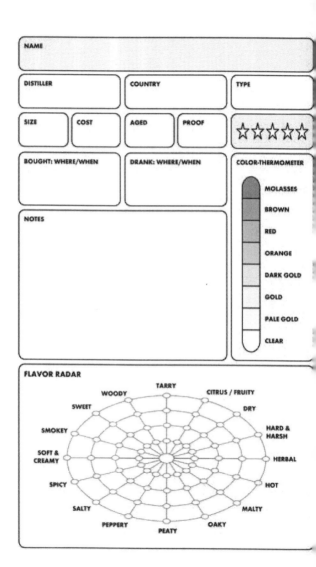

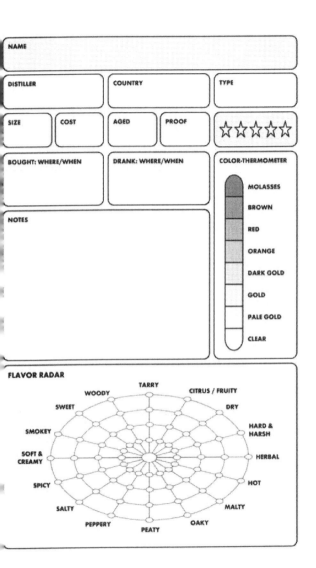

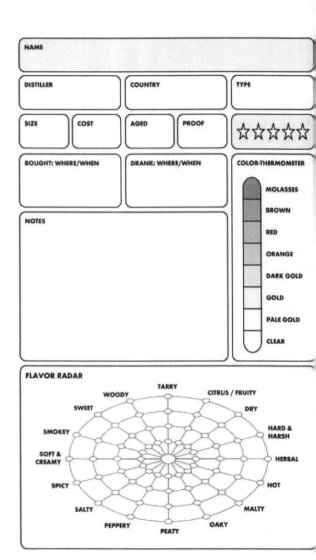

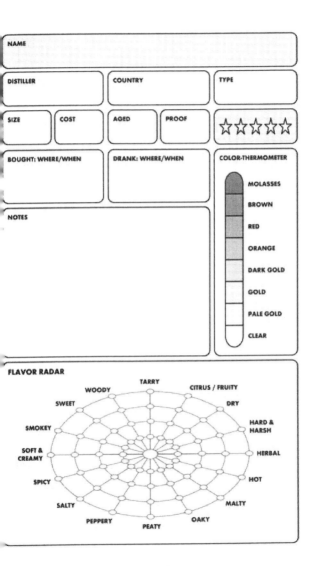

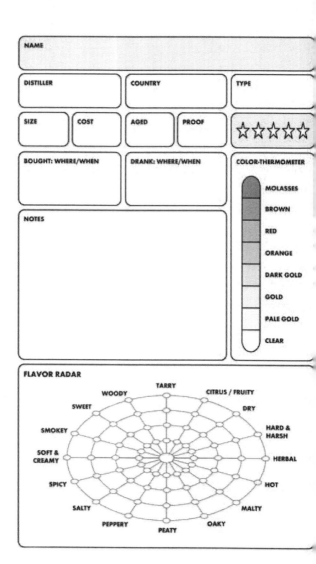

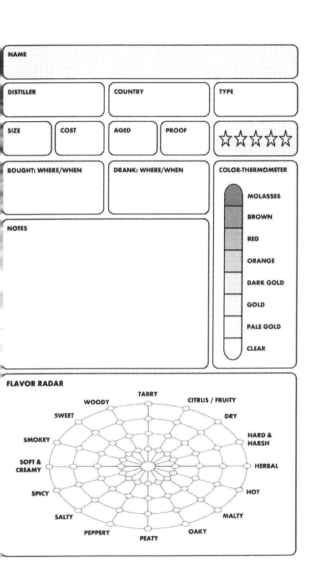

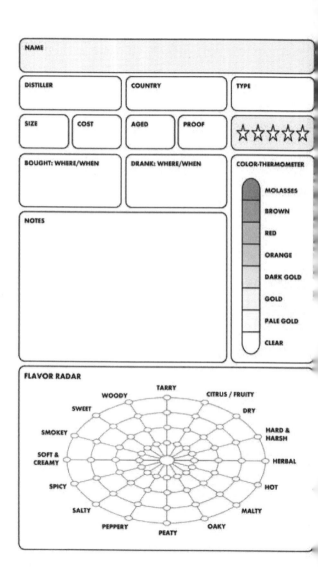

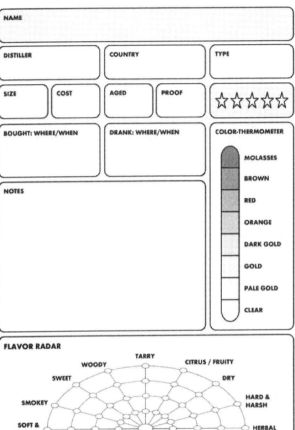

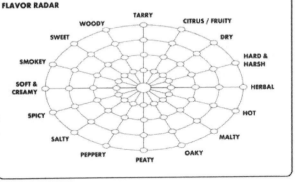

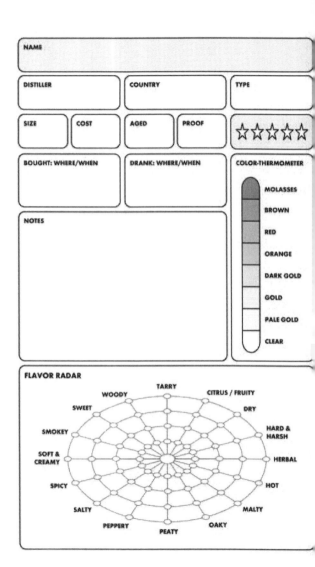

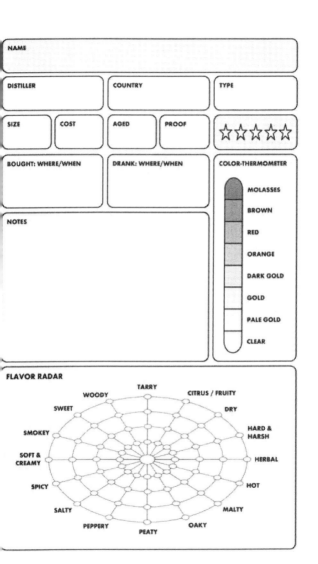

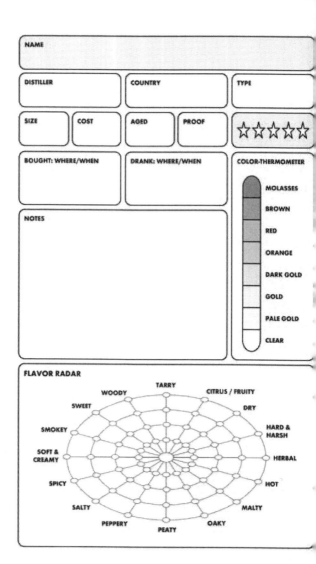

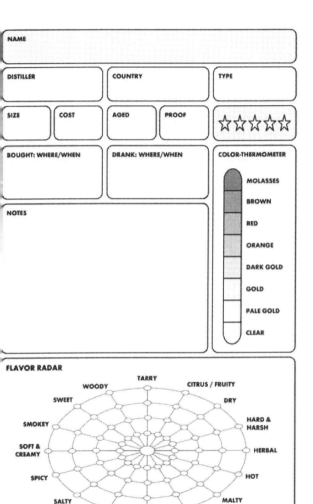

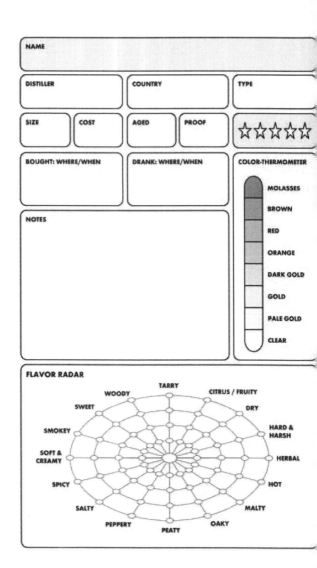

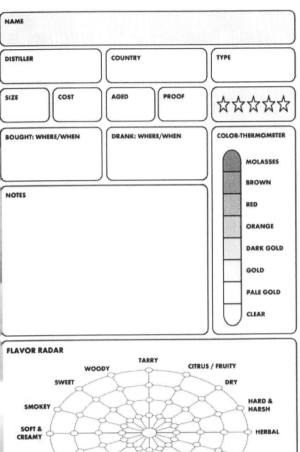

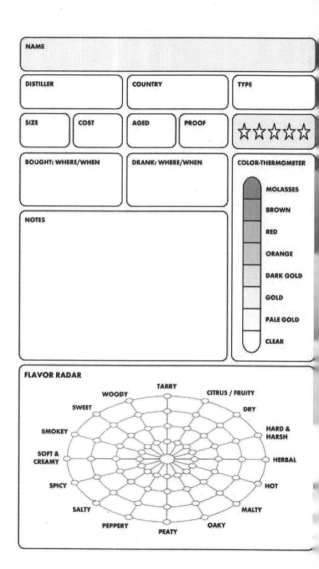

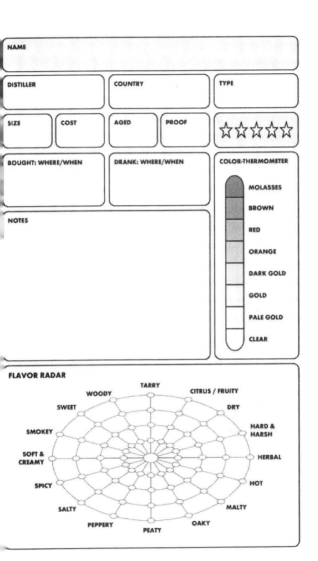

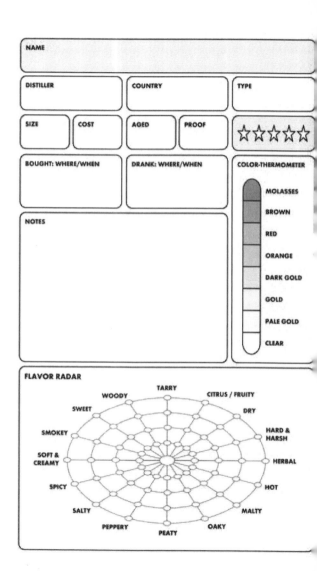

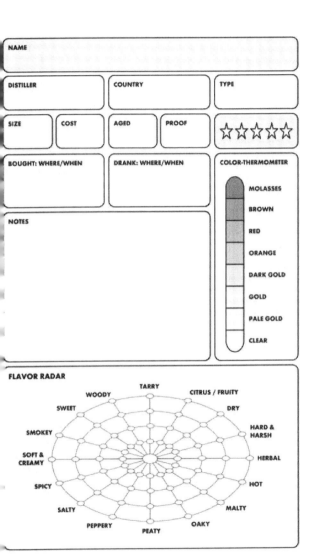

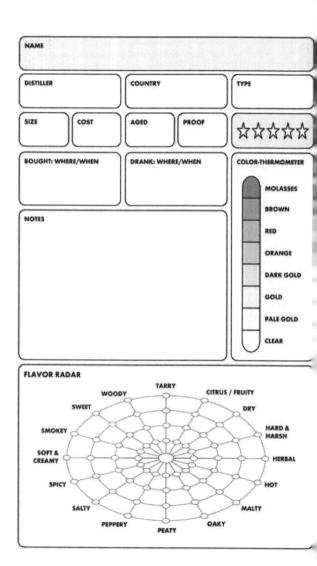

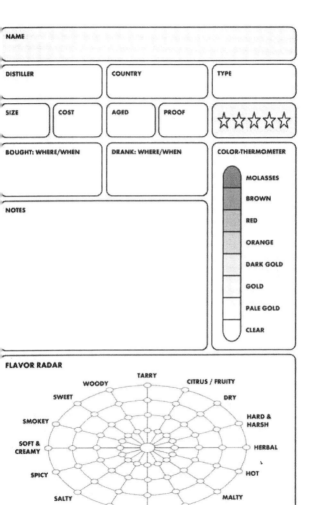

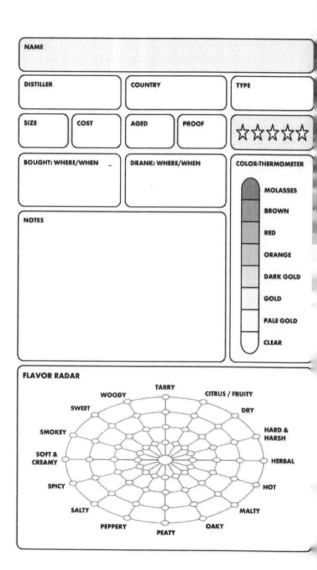

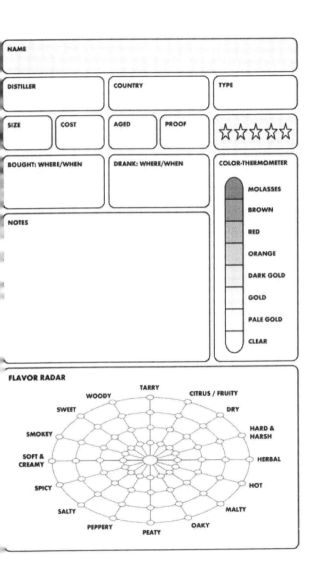

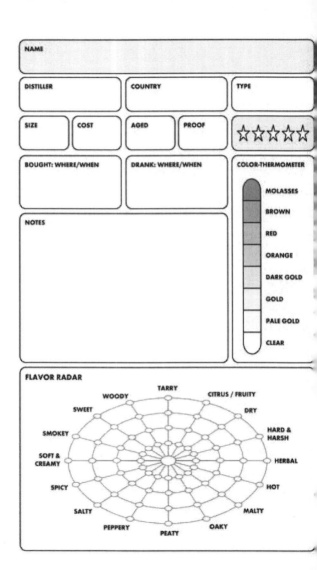

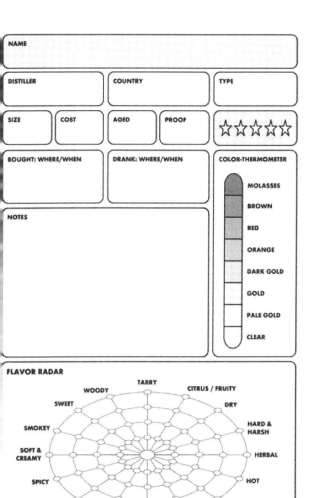

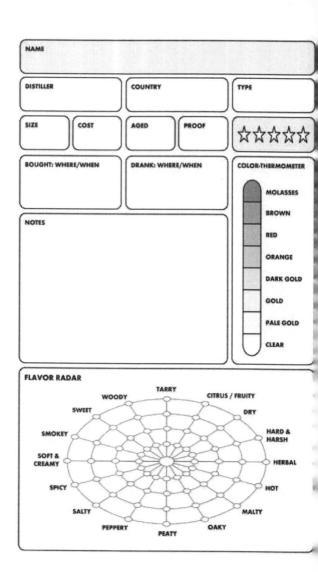

Printed in Great Brita
by Amazon.co.uk, L
Marston Gate.